"Now the God of peace, who brought up from the dead the great Shepherd of the sheep through the blood of the eternal Covenant, even Jesus our Lord, equip you in every good thing to do His will, working in us that which is pleasing in His sight, through Jesus Christ, to whom be the glory forever and ever. Amen.

Hebrews 13:20-21

Love in the Great Shepherd,

Don & Elisabeth Hoffman
Maria, Aaron, Ben,
Paige & Beth Anne

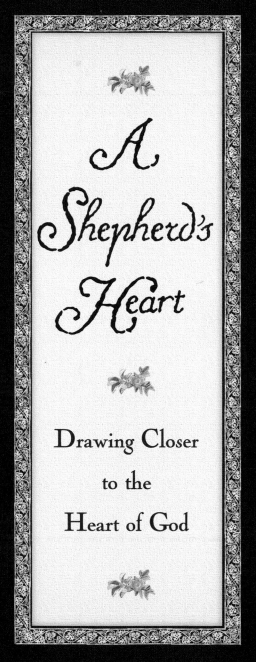

A Shepherd's Heart

Drawing Closer
to the
Heart of God

Illustrations

A Shepherd's Heart

Written & Compiled by
Paul C. Brownlow

Brownlow

Contents

Foreword

A Shepherd's Heart is a compilation of essays and brief thoughts, poems and Scripture verses that narrate and explore the Biblical imagery of sheep and a shepherd. Some are from my favorite authors, including my dad, Leroy Brownlow. Some are from my own hand and heart. And while a few of the essays cover the same fertile ground (Psalm 23 and others), each brings a treasured and unique insight of inspiration.

The magnificent illustrations, carefully chosen over several years, are from selected museums and private collections around the world. We gratefully thank their curators and owners for these masterpieces and for helping to create this unique book.

It is my hope that we all will savor these short glimpses of God's shepherd love. It is His abiding desire that we follow His call and allow Him to create shepherd hearts that beat within us all.   P.C.B.

Trust in the Lord and do good; dwell in the land and enjoy safe pasture.

PSALM 37.3

A Shepherd's Heart

God's favorite image for Himself and us is that of the shepherd and the sheep. This beautiful analogy has lost some of its power today because we know so little about sheep. We know more about computer wizards and hockey players than we do sheep. But the more we learn about sheep—how pitiful, completely passive, helpless and dumb they are—the more fitting and appropriate the metaphor becomes.

While God is the Great Shepherd and Christ the Good Shepherd, they never intended to be the only shepherds. As we all know, God planned that leaders be selected as shepherds in every church. However, the task of shepherding and tending sheep was not designed to stop even there. It is my belief that God intended for us all to be shepherds in a way, for us *all* to have a shepherd's heart.

When we listen to God's Word, we are told to care for each other:

> *Be devoted to one another in brotherly love.*
> *Honor one another above yourselves.*
>
> ROMANS 12:10

> *Each of you should look not only to his*
> *own interests, but also the interests of others.*
>
> PHILIPPIANS 2:4

> *Carry one another's burdens.*
>
> GALATIANS 6:12

So when the Apostle Paul tells us to be imitators of God (Ephesians 5:1), he is telling us to imitate a shepherd, to look like shepherds, to act like shepherds, to think like shepherds, to have a shepherd's heart.

While there are numerous passages that describe God as a shepherd, my favorite is from the poet/prophet Isaiah:

> *He tends his flock like a shepherd:*
> *He gathers the lambs in his arms*
> *And carries them close to his heart;*
> *he gently leads those that have young.*
>
> ISAIAH 40:11

I love this simple picture. It is the story of a shepherd leading his flock to higher ground. The old mother ewe with her lamb is having trouble keeping up. It is difficult terrain—the rocks are large, the thorns that tear and pierce her flesh are sharp, the climb is steep.

In the midst of this difficult journey she knows that if she falls too far behind, the wolf or hawk will feast upon her and her tender lamb. She wants to keep up, she knows she needs to go on, she wants to follow but just cannot.

What does the shepherd do now? Does he scold her for being weak? Does he angrily announce his intentions to find some "better" sheep? No. He stops, reaches down, cradles the lamb and puts him inside his tunic. There the lamb is safe, there he knows he is protected, there he can feel the beating of the shepherd's heart. At this point, the shepherd pats the old mother ewe on the head and gently encourages her with the words, "Come with me. We can make it." And at a slower but steady pace, they together renew their climb to higher ground.

This is what God does for us. That is what we are called to do for each other: to nurture and encourage, to show compassion and concern, to let those around us feel the beating of our hearts.

God not only hears our words,
He listens to our hearts.
ANONYMOUS

One loving heart sets another on fire.
AUGUSTINE

The widest thing in the universe is not space;
it is the potential capacity of the human heart.
Being made in the image of God, it is capable
of almost unlimited extension in all directions.
And one of the world's greatest tragedies is
that we allow our hearts to shrink until there
is room in them for little beside themselves.
A. W. TOZER

Nothing is impossible to the willing heart.
THOMAS HEYWOOD

Our heart is in heaven,
our home is not here.

REGINALD HEBER

Beside Still Waters

When we follow the Shepherd, we will get to where He is going. And our Shepherd is going to a place of peace and rest beside still waters. However, the path to the pasture is not always smooth or easy. We are told it is filled with torrents of tribulation, barren hills and enemies on every side. Life here is not always a pleasant walk in a garden paradise. It is a journey home where we will be at rest, blessed with the fellowship and friendship of our God forever.

The Promised Land always lies
on the other side of a wilderness.

HAVELOCK ELLIS

No one will go to heaven who has not
sent his heart there before him.

THOMAS WILSON

This world is but the vestibule of eternity.
Every good thought or deed touches
a chord that vibrates in heaven.

ANONYMOUS

Those are dead even for this life
who hope for no other.

JOHANN WOLFGANG VON GOETHE

Children
are
messengers
we send
to a time
we will
not see.

The Children's Psalm

*P*erhaps it is time that we all get back to the nursery again, and take up our childish verses once more and, while reading them with the intelligence of our grown-up years, to believe them with all our old childish faith.

Let me carry you back then to The Children's Psalm, that one which is so universally taught to the little ones in the nursery and in the infant school. Do we not each remember the Twenty-third Psalm as long as we can remember anything? And, can we not recall even now something of the joy and pride our childish hearts felt when first we were able to repeat it? Since then we have always known it, but perhaps its words sound so old and familiar to us now that we cannot see the meaning they convey.

But in truth, these words tell us the whole story of our faith. They bring such wondrous depth of meaning that I doubt it has ever entered into any heart to conceive the things they reveal.

Let us now repeat these familiar words to ourselves afresh:

The Lord is my shepherd: I shall not want.

He maketh me to lie down in green pastures: he leadeth me beside the still waters.

He restoreth my soul: he leadeth me in the paths of righteousness for his name's sake.

Yea, though I walk through the valley of the shadow of death, I will fear no evil: for thou art with me: thy rod and thy staff they comfort me.

Thou preparest a table before me in the presence of mine enemies: thou anointest my head with oil: my cup runneth over.

Surely goodness and mercy shall follow me all the days of my life: and I will dwell in the house of the Lord for ever.

HANNAH WHITALL SMITH

Since my youth, O God, you have taught me, and to this day I declare your marvelous deeds.

PSALM 71:17

The spirituality of a child depends on what its mother and father are, and not on what they say.

HENRI FRÉDÉRIC AMIEL

How great is the love the Father has lavished on us, that we should be called children of God! And that is what we are!

1 JOHN 3:1

A Shepherd's Compassion

He who has compassion on them will guide them and lead them beside springs of water.

ISAIAH 49:10

Our God is an inherently compassionate God. As grapevines produce grapes and fruit trees produce fruit, it is His nature to show compassion.

God is full of compassion. It is not a sideline quality He has tried to cultivate. Neither is He a miserly master doling it out when forced to do so. From His heavenly vault, God "crowns us with love and compassion" (Psalm 103:4). We are fitted with royal robes of grace and mercy, and then He confers a crown of love and compassion on our brow. It is a king's wardrobe, and it is bestowed on us!

As followers of a compassionate Shepherd, we become compassionate people. It will be our normal response, we will be "clothed with compassion" (Colossians 3:12). Now clothing is part of our everyday life. It is not a happenstance event—some days on, some days off. Just as we do not decide each morning if we will wear clothes or not, the decision for compassion is not a daily one. It is our very nature; we are naked without it, and it becomes part of us.

Often misunderstood, compassion is not a passive thing like sorrow or pity. It is possible to feel a great deal of sorrow and pity for a person, yet do nothing. True compassion will have none of these passive passions. Compassion senses the deep hurt without waiting to be told. Compassion feels another's pain in its own heart. But compassion, if it be true, is not complete with just feelings. Compassion acts to relieve the anguish and soothe the hurt.

Our Lord modeled this three-part compassion for us. Visiting village after village, Jesus saw the people and had "compassion on them, because they were harassed and helpless, like sheep without a shepherd" (Matthew 9:36). Jesus sensed their plight and wept. But tears were not enough. In a final act of compassion, He redeemed both them and us.

As sheep of the Good Shepherd and undershepherds to each other, our compassion will not stop at sorrow or tears, but will daily act to bring comfort to those around us.

Pity weeps and runs away;
Compassion comes to help and stay.

JANET CURTIS O'LEARY

I never ask the wounded person how he feels;
I myself become the wounded person.

WALT WHITMAN

Man may dismiss compassion from his heart,
but God will never.

WILLIAM COWPER

The Cry of the Lamb

Once a friend of mine was visiting a sheep farm in Australia. The owner of the farm took a young lamb and placed it in a huge enclosure where there were several thousand sheep whose bleating, together with the shouting of the sheep-shearers, was deafening. Then the lamb uttered its feeble cry, and the mother sheep at the other end of the enclosure heard it and started to find her lamb.

Do not ever imagine that we are beyond the reach of the Good Shepherd. He sees us, He hears us; every good desire of ours is known to Him, and every secret longing for better things. He sees and hears us as if there were no other child in the world!

P. T. FORSYTH

LAMB OF GOD

The next day John saw Jesus coming toward him and said, "Look, the Lamb of God, who takes away the sin of the world!"
JOHN 1:39

When they had finished eating, Jesus said to Simon Peter, "Simon son of John, do you truly love me more than these?" "Yes, Lord," he said, "you know that I love you." Jesus said, "Feed my lambs."
JOHN 21:15

Whispers of His Love

In Scripture, a man had a hundred sheep, lost one of them, and went after it. And when he had found the runaway, laid it on his shoulders and travelled home. This wasn't a very comfortable position for the sheep, held on by the legs with its head hanging down. That's the way the Lord carries old sheep when we go astray.

But the lambs He carries in His bosom. The shoulder is not for them, but the bosom. There they lie, with His arms folded about them—there, where His kind eye can keep its glance upon them. In His bosom, where they can feel the great full heart beating in its love, where He can hear the first mutter of their fear, and they can catch the gentlest whisper of His loving care. He carries them in His bosom.

Close to Him, cradled in His arms, we are sustained and safe.

M. GUY PEARSE

IF I WERE A SHEPHERD

What can I give Him, poor as I am?
If I were a shepherd, I would bring a lamb;
If I were a wise man, I would do my part;
Yet what I can I give Him—
Give my heart.

CHRISTINA GEORGINA ROSSETTI

A Shepherd's Faith

Shepherds and sheep share so much of the same life and similar surroundings. They share the same path, the same sun, the same heat, the same thorns and rocks, the same peaceful valleys and cool streams.

But they don't share the same vision. Sheep are really nearsighted, both physically and mentally. They see only the grass in front of them, unaware of the dangers that surround or the distant hills that beckon.

The shepherd sees things that sheep never dream of. Abraham—our patriarch and early pattern—saw things that were not, as though they were. But it was not Abraham's eyes that gave him eternal vision; it was his faith. And so it is for us.

When our faith is strong, we see the unseen and accomplish the impossible. We can encourage and nurture our fellow sheep to continue the climb for higher ground when we, by word or deed, faithfully remind them:

> There is a God. He is real and He cares.
> We only have to trust.
>
> There is an answer to life's problems.
> To turn our lives over to one more powerful
> than we is not to be weak.
>
> There is a hope for a better life.
> This is but an overnight stay in a roadside cottage.
> This is not our home.

Faith gives vision to our eyes and fills them with hope.

Faith is a grasping of Almighty power; the hand of man laid on the arm of God, the grand and blessed hour in which the things impossible to me become the possible, O Lord, through Thee.

A. E. HAMILTON

When people stop believing in God they do not believe in nothing. They believe in anything.

G. K. CHESTERTON

Faith is simply the welcome of the one who says, "Here I am." And taking that as our starting point, we can be on our way.

JACQUES ELLUL

Faith is a living, daring confidence in God's grace, so sure and certain that a man could stake his life on it a thousand times.

MARTIN LUTHER

Little faith will bring your soul to heaven; great faith will bring heaven to your soul.

CHARLES H. SPURGEON

It is of the essence of faith to let God be God.

JON SOBRINO

Worthy Is the Lamb

Near the top of the steeple of an old church in Norway, a small lamb is carved. It was not put there for elaborate decoration, but from deepest gratitude.

As the church was being built, a worker high on the tower scaffold lost his balance and fell to the ground. The other workers knew he would be dead, but hurried quickly down to his side. To their amazement and joyful surprise, the man was not dead. He was only slightly injured and was alive!

Just before his fall, a flock of sheep wandered close to the new church on their way to pasture. The worker fell on a lamb that cushioned his fall. He was saved, but the lamb was crushed to death.

Later in tribute and honor, a craftsman climbed to the top of the tower and carved a small lamb in stone at the exact place from which the workman fell.

Saved by the lamb. Who among us cannot say the same!

RICK ATCHLEY

Worthy is the lamb who was slain to receive power and wealth and wisdom and strength and honor and glory and praise!

REVELATION 5:12

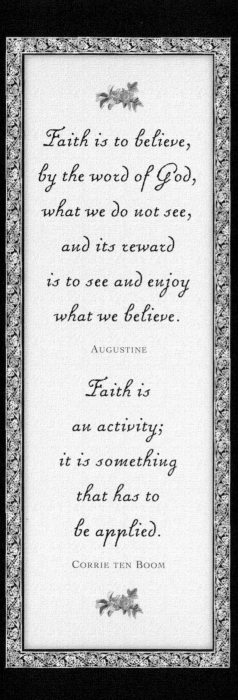

Faith is to believe,
by the word of God,
what we do not see,
and its reward
is to see and enjoy
what we believe.

AUGUSTINE

Faith is
an activity;
it is something
that has to
be applied.

CORRIE TEN BOOM

The great
act of faith
is when man
decides that
he is not God.

O. W. HOLMES, JR.

Let us not go faster
than God. It is
our emptiness
and our thirst
that He needs,
not our plenitude.

JACQUES MARITAIN

An Earlier Heaven

There seems to have been a sense in which David enjoyed heaven before he got there. To him the Lord's house was not simply a thing of the future, but a possibility for the present. In another psalm he talks of dwelling in the secret place of the Most High, and in yet another he employs the noble words, "One thing have I desired of the Lord, that will I seek after; that I may dwell in the house of the Lord all the days of my life, to behold the beauty of the Lord, and to inquire in his temple" (Psalm 27:4).

We have no doubt that his fervent prayer was answered and that the fixed purpose of his heart found its ideal. Whether at home in the palace of Mount Zion, or away in the desolate wastes beyond Jordan, David did dwell in the house of the Lord, beholding His beauty and inquiring His will. What is the house of God but the presence of God, habitually recognized by the loving and believing spirit.

Why should we not also begin to live in the house of God, in this hallowed and blessed sense? Our heaven may thus begin, not at the moment we first enter the gates of the city, but the day when we first wash our robes and make them white in the blood of the Lamb. Always and everywhere we may find our dwelling in God, who has been the home and refuge and abiding place of His people in all generations. Always and everywhere we may retreat into Him from the windy storm and tempest. May the Holy Spirit make real to each of us this possibility of living in the house of the Lord hourly and daily; where all tears are wiped as soon as shed; where cares cannot invade; and where the Good Shepherd leads His flock ever into green pastures.

F. B. Meyer

His People, His Sheep

Make a joyful noise unto the Lord, all ye lands.
Serve the Lord with gladness:
come before his presence with singing.
Know ye that the Lord he is God:
it is he that hath made us, and not we ourselves;
we are his people, and the sheep of his pasture.
Enter into his gates with thanksgiving,
and into his courts with praise:
be thankful unto him, and bless his name.
For the Lord is good; his mercy is everlasting;
and his truth endureth to all generations.

Psalm 100

Of Sheep and Shepherds

Throughout Victorian times, the Cotswold region of England was a leisurely large expanse of gently rolling hills with charming cottages and pastures of placid sheep. It was a sight that inspired painters and poets, young milk maidens and elderly matrons.

Now these serene grassy hills were not anything like the Middle Eastern environment that shepherds contended with to protect their sheep. The ancient shepherd was a warrior, scout and protector earning his livelihood in a way that was anything but "romantic" or "charming."

But we all know people are about the same from one time period to another, and so are sheep. They are helpless animals in constant need of a shepherd. We are human, we have seasons of joy mixed with pain. We hope, we dream, we build. We make mistakes and suffer the consequences. We too need a shepherd.

It was David the shepherd boy made king who in later life was to set forth the immortal words we have all cherished since childhood:

> *The Lord is my shepherd.*
> *I shall not want.*
>
> PSALM 23:1

Now it is one thing for children to know this famous psalm. (I first quoted the entire Twenty-third Psalm when I was three years old to the assembled crowd at the church where my father preached.) It is quite another thing to understand and fathom the depth of such a statement.

It takes a lifetime to learn the full and finer meaning of these simple words—just as it took David a lifetime of living finally to be able to compose them.

God tells us we are sheep, but not just any sheep. We are His sheep:

> *Know that the Lord is God. It is he who made us, and we are his; we are his people, the sheep of his pasture.*
>
> PSALM 100:3

> *He brought his people out like a flock;*
> *he led them like sheep through the desert.*
>
> PSALM 78:52

We could have no more exalted place or position of privilege than to be the sheep of God's pasture. And that is what we are!

> *God chose David his servant*
> *and took him from the sheep pens;*
> *from tending sheep he brought him*
> *to be the shepherd of his people.*

> *And David shepherded them*
> *with integrity of heart;*
> *with skillful hands he led them.*
>
> PSALM 78:70-72

He will stand and shepherd his flock
in the strength of the Lord.

MICAH 5:4

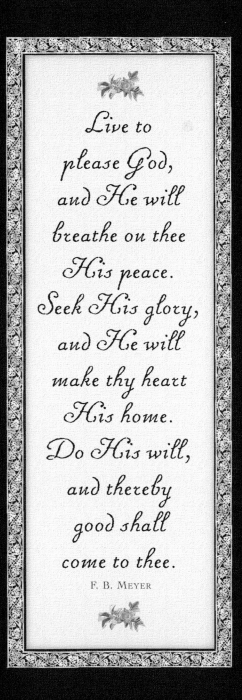

Live to
please God,
and He will
breathe on thee
His peace.
Seek His glory,
and He will
make thy heart
His home.
Do His will,
and thereby
good shall
come to thee.

F. B. MEYER

Cups of Blessing

Glad and joyous moments come to even the weariest of hearts. In such blessed hours, life is a cup mixed by the loving hand of God, overflowing with mercy and loving-kindness.

Besides the blessings of health, the sweet affections of close friendships, the joys of family and home, God sends now and then an extra sweetness—some special deliverance, some unexpected benevolence, some undeserved benefit—sent apparently for no other reason than to satisfy God's passion for giving.

But whatever blessing is in our cup, it is sure to run over. With Him the calf is always fattened; the robe is always the best; the joy is unspeakable; the peace passes understanding; the grace is so abundant that we have all sufficiency for all things, and abound in every good work. God does not measure out His goodness as the apothecary counts his drops and measures his potions slowly and exactly, drop by drop. God's way is always characterized by plenteous abundance and overflowing bounty.

Spiritual blessings, however, are the ones our cups most often overflow, and discerning eyes see God's spiritual benevolence everywhere. In one of his seasons of rapt communion with God, a Scottish believer cried, "O Lord, cease Thy blessings; it is enough. I am only a clay vessel and can contain no more!"

Our Lord meant us to have the abiding experience of such joys because He not only came to give us life, but life more abundantly. He spoke to us His unmistakable words that our joy might be full. He meant our hearts to delight themselves with fullness, and to be satisfied with the favor of the Lord.

Let us not hoard what we have been given. Let us freely permit our cups to run over. Far from us to be the miser who dares not give because he fears he will not get. Let us be generous with our wealth; for we know that it is inexhaustible, being supplied from our Father's hand.

F. B. MEYER

The Lord gives His blessing when He finds the vessel empty.

THOMAS À KEMPIS

The greatest blessing we ever get from God is to know that we are destitute spiritually.

OSWALD CHAMBERS

All that is required to make men unmindful of what they owe to God for any blessing is that they should receive that blessing often and regularly.

RICHARD WHATELY

Once it was the blessing, now it is the Lord.

ALBERT BENJAMIN SIMPSON

The Shepherd and His Flock

"I tell you the truth, the man who does not enter the sheep pen by the gate, but climbs in by some other way, is a thief and a robber. The man who enters by the gate is the shepherd of his sheep. The watchman opens the gate for him, and the sheep listen to his voice. He calls his own sheep by name and leads them out. When he has brought out all his own, he goes on ahead of them, and his sheep follow him because they know his voice. But they will never follow a stranger; in fact, they will run away from him because they do not recognize a stranger's voice." Jesus used this figure of speech, but they did not understand what he was telling them.

Therefore Jesus said again, "I tell you the truth, I am the gate for the sheep. All who ever came before me were thieves and robbers, but the sheep did not listen to them. I am the gate; whoever enters through me will be saved. He will come in and go out, and find pasture. The thief comes only to steal and kill and destroy; I have come that they may have life, and have it to the full.

"I am the good shepherd. The good shepherd lays down his life for the sheep. The hired hand is not the shepherd who owns the sheep. So when he sees the wolf coming, he abandons the sheep and runs away. Then the wolf attacks the flock and scatters it. The man runs away because he is a hired hand and cares nothing for the sheep.

"I am the good shepherd; I know my sheep and my sheep know me—just as the Father knows me and I know the Father—and I lay down my life for the sheep. I have other sheep that are not of this flock. I must bring them also. They too will listen to my voice, and there shall be one flock and one shepherd."

JOHN 10:1–16

A Shepherd's Comfort

The shepherd is trained not to be concerned with his own comfort. His job is often very uncomfortable—when strays must be brought back, when enemies must be rebuffed, when sleep must be postponed in order to guard his flock. His role is to think of comforting those in his care, not himself.

As the sheep of God, we have all been divinely comforted. The Apostle Paul himself clearly told us:

> *Thank God that the Great Shepherd of all comfort and compassion has comforted us poor sheep so that we can show comfort to the other sheep around us.*
>
> PARAPHRASE OF 2 CORINTHIANS 1:3, 4

We have been the blessed recipients of God's benevolence, not so we can gather it up for our own contentment, but so we can joyously and freely distribute it to others. We have been comforted to comfort, blessed to bless, loved to love.

If I can put one touch of rosy sunset into the life of any man or woman, I shall feel that I have worked with God.

GEORGE MACDONALD

I used to ask God to help me. Then I asked if I might help Him. I ended up by asking Him to do His work through me.

HUDSON TAYLOR

This is well-nigh the greatest of discoveries a man can make, that God is not confined in churches, but that the streets are sacred because His presence is there, that the market-place is one of His abiding places, and ought, therefore, to be a sanctuary. Any moment in any place, the veil can suddenly grow thin and God be seen.

R. C. GILLIE

I find the doing of the will of God leaves me no time for disputing about His plans.

GEORGE MACDONALD

Are we not one? Are we not joined by heaven? Each interwoven with the other's fate?

ANONYMOUS

God does not comfort us to make us comfortable, but to make us comforters.

JOHN HENRY JOWETT

If this is God's world, there are no unimportant people.

GEORGE THOMAS

No one is useless in this world who lightens the burden of it for anyone else.

CHARLES DICKENS

Come, let us bow down in worship, let us kneel before the Lord our Maker; For he is God and we are the people of his pasture, the flock under his care.

PSALM 95:6, 7

Even the Best

The anonymous poet who composed Psalm 119 (an acrostic poem of praise) spoke for us all when he said in the last verse of this, the longest psalm:

I have strayed like a lost sheep.
Seek your servant, for I have not
forgotten your commands.

The psalmist is really saying, "Lord, I haven't forgotten You, I'm doing the best I can. But I'm helpless, help me. I'm lost, find me!"

It is good sometimes to remember that even the most devoted sheep are helpless and lost at times. The best sheep are not the ones who know all about pleasant pastures and vicious predators. The best sheep are the ones who know how much they need a shepherd.

How blest are those who know they are sheep,
who know their need for a Shepherd.

PARAPHRASE OF MATTHEW 5:3

Take glory neither in money, if you have some,
nor in influential friends, but in God
who gives you everything and above all
wants to give you Himself.

THOMAS À KEMPIS

It is from out of the depths of our humility that
the height of our destiny looks grandest.
Let me truly feel that in myself I am nothing,
and at once, through every inlet of my soul,
God comes in, and is everything in me.

WILLIAM MOUNTFORD

We mount to heaven mostly on the ruins of our
cherished schemes, finding our failures were successes.

AMOS BRONSON ALCOTT

Yet for all God's good will toward us,
He is unable to grant us our heart's desires till
all our desires have been reduced to one.

A. W. TOZER

It is only imperfection that complains of what is
imperfect. The more perfect we are, the more gentle
and quiet we become toward the defects of others.

FRANÇOIS FÉNELON

A Shepherd's Love

Love is at the root of even the earthly shepherd's care for his flock, if he is a true shepherd, and not just a hireling. Without love, there may be care but it will not be tender care; there may be protection but it will not be incessant, unwearied protection.

The heavenly Shepherd loves the sheep of His flock with a deep, true, patient, and abounding love—far surpassing our utmost affection, surpassing even the utmost conception that we can form of love. His flock is his own creation, His own reflected image, His own purchased possession. His desire is toward it. He loves it with a love which "many waters cannot quench, neither can the floods drown."

God loves His flock. And if we have a shepherd's heart, we will love His flock as well.

ANONYMOUS

Take away love and our earth is a tomb.

ROBERT BROWNING

Our Lord does not care so much for the importance of our works as for the love with which they are done.

TERESA OF AVILA

The first duty of love is to listen.

PAUL TILLICH

Hearts that are open to the love that is God, feel loved in loving and served in serving

EDWARD GLOEGGLER

We have a God who loves.
That means that we have a God who suffers.

J. B. PHILLIPS

We shall one day forget all about duty, and do everything from the love of the loveliness of it, the satisfaction of the rightness of it.

GEORGE MACDONALD

Human things must be known to be loved: but divine things must be loved to be known.

BLAISE PASCAL

I praise the Lord because he has shown his wonderful love to me.

PSALM 31:21

There is only one being who loves perfectly, and that is God, yet the New Testament distinctly states that we are to love as God does; so the first step is obvious. If ever we are going to have perfect love in our hearts we must have the very nature of God in us.

OSWALD CHAMBERS

The great
acts of love
are done
by those
who are
habitually
performing
small acts
of kindness.

God is great,
and therefore
He will
be sought:
God is good,
and therefore
He will
be found.

People of the Pasture

While the Shepherd has much to do, the part of the sheep is very simple. It is only to trust and to follow. The Shepherd does all the rest. He leads the sheep by the right way. He chooses their paths for them and sees that they are paths where the sheep can walk in safety. When He moves the sheep, He goes before them. The sheep have none of the planning to do, none of the decisions to make, none of the forethought or wisdom to exercise; they have absolutely nothing to do but to trust themselves entirely to the care of the Good Shepherd, and to follow Him wherever He leads. It is very simple. There is nothing complicated in trusting, when the One we are called upon to trust is absolutely trustworthy; and nothing complicated in obedience, when we have perfect confidence in the power we are obeying.

Let us then begin to trust and to follow our Shepherd here and now. Let us abandon ourselves to His care and guidance, as a sheep in the care of a shepherd, and trust Him completely.

We need not be afraid to follow, for He always leads His sheep into green pastures and beside still waters. No matter that we may seem to be in the very midst of a desert, with nothing green about us inwardly or outwardly and we may think we will have to journey far before we can get to green pastures. The Good Shepherd can turn the very place where we are into green pastures. He has power to make the desert rejoice and blossom as the rose; and He has promised that "in the wilderness shall waters break out, and streams in the desert."

HANNAH WHITALL SMITH

Save your people and bless your inheritance;
be their shepherd and carry them forever.

PSALM 28:9

There are times when God asks nothing
of His children except silence, patience, and tears.

CHARLES SEYMOUR ROBINSON

God is not in the slightest degree baffled or bewildered
by what baffles and bewilders us. . . . He is either
a present help or He is not much help at all.

J. B. PHILLIPS

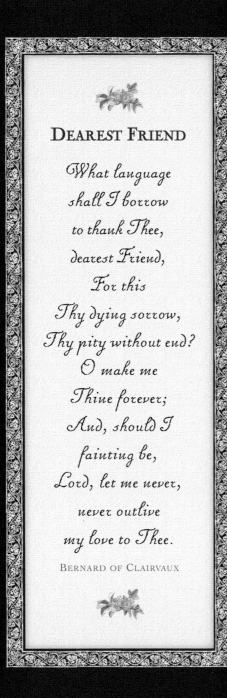

DEAREST FRIEND

*What language
shall I borrow
to thank Thee,
dearest Friend,
For this
Thy dying sorrow,
Thy pity without end?
O make me
Thine forever;
And, should I
fainting be,
Lord, let me never,
never outlive
my love to Thee.*

BERNARD OF CLAIRVAUX

Our Shepherd Friend

Shepherd—that precious word for God was uttered first by Jacob (himself once a shepherd) as he lay dying. Looking back on his long journey, Jacob praised God—the one "who has been my shepherd all my life." All through the Bible the golden thread runs, until in its closing pages we read of the Lamb who leads His flock to glory.

The Eastern shepherd occupied quite a unique position toward his flock, and a friendship sprang up between him and the dumb creatures of his care to which there is no counterpart among ourselves.

In the early morning he would lead his flock from their fold to the pasture lands. All day he must closely watch, lest harm should come to them from prowling beasts or robbers. To the still waters he must lead them, that they may drink where no swift current shall frighten them. And at night he must conduct them back to the security of the fold. At a certain seasons of the year he must lead them yet farther afield, far away from his own home and the haunts of men, where he will live among them, scorched by the heat at noon and drenched by the dews at night.

Should one of the lambs be unable to keep pace with the rest of the flock he must carry it in his bosom. Should one of his flock go astray he must search for it until he finds it, tracking it by the tufts of wool left in the briers and thorns. Should danger assail he must be prepared to risk his life. Shepherds in the East look like warriors armed for fight—the gun slung over the shoulder, pistols at the belt, and club in hand.

Living on such terms, the shepherd and his flock are almost friends. They know him and answer to their names. Some always follow close behind him, as his special favorites, sure of his love. He can do almost as he wills with any of them, going freely in and out among them without exciting the slightest symptom of alarm.

Now all this is true of our Lord Jesus, that Great Shepherd of the sheep. He has a shepherd's heart, beating with pure and generous love that counted not His life-blood too dear a price to pay for our ransom. He has a shepherd's eye, that takes in the whole flock, and misses not even the poor sheep wandering away on the mountains cold. He has a shepherd's faithfulness, which will never fail nor forsake, nor leave us comfortless, nor flee when He sees the wolf coming. He has a shepherd's strength, so that He is well able to deliver us from the jaw of the lion or the paw of the bear. He has a shepherd's tenderness—no lamb so tiny that He will not carry it; no saint so weak that He will not gently lead; no soul so faint that He will not give it rest. He pities as a father. He comforts as a mother. His gentleness makes great. He covers us with His feathers, soft and warm and downy; and under His wings do we trust.

But, He has done more! "All we like sheep have gone astray," said the prophet Isaiah. Punishment and disaster were imminent; but Jesus, from His throne in eternity, saw the danger and was filled with compassion for us who were as sheep without a shepherd. Therefore, because He was the Shepherd, He laid down His life for the sheep, and thus redeemed the flock by the blood of the everlasting covenant.

Let us praise God that we have a Shepherd, and that amid all the sorrow and want of the world, the Lord's sheep are well supplied.

F. B. Meyer

No one has a right to look with contempt on himself when God has shown such an interest in him.

The Lord Is My Shepherd

Picture ourselves in the Middle East. The sun is radiant-hot. The earth is scorched dry. We see a few wobbly sheep nibbling at burnt grass already bitten too close to the disappointing ground. Sheep without food, without water, without future. But wait! There is more to the picture. Our view broadens, and we see the shepherd standing nearby. His existence is as real as the sheep. And his presence, power, and providence change everything. The presence of the shepherd! That made all the difference for the sheep, and it can do the same for us.

LEROY BROWNLOW

It is good for us to know, as certainly as
David did, that we belong to the Lord.
There is no "if" nor "but," nor even "I hope so."
But he says, "The Lord is my shepherd."
We must cultivate this same spirit of
assured dependence upon our heavenly Father.
If He be a Shepherd to no one else,
He is a Shepherd to me. He cares for me,
watches over me, and preserves me.

CHARLES H. SPURGEON

Children
are the
hands by
which we
take hold
of heaven.

HENRY WARD BEECHER

The Lambs Among Us

Lambs are the youngest, the most fragile of the flock. They are constantly watched by the mother ewe, the shepherd—and yes, the wolf. Because of their inexperience and extreme vulnerability, the shepherd treats them with special care.

We too have young ones who need a wise and gentle shepherd. And accordingly, we lavish them with tender love, knowing what to overlook, and when gently to guide and direct.

While our own children are the first ones we think of, are there not other lambs among us—children and young people in our neighborhoods and in our churches—that we can gently nurture and encourage?

Just as all babies are born with a great need for love that they never outgrow, all of us, lambs and sheep alike, are born with a need for encouragement that never tires of its expression. How easy it is done, how mighty is its impact. Encouragement is oxygen to the soul and revives tender hearts.

God tempers the wind to the shorn lamb.

ENGLISH PROVERB

The right instruction of youth is a matter in which Christ and the whole world is concerned.

MARTIN LUTHER

God commanded our forefathers to teach their children, so the next generation would know them [His statutes], even the children yet to be born, and they in turn would tell their children. Then they would put their trust in God and not forget his deeds.

PSALM 78:5–7

What we desire our children to become, we must endeavor to be before them.

ANDREW COMBE

My hands are too tired to hold a torch on high, but they can light a candle in a nursery.

ELLIS MEREDITH

Let parents bequeath to their children not riches, but the spirit of reverence.

PLATO

From the lips of children and infants you have ordained praise.

PSALM 8:2

I love little children, and it is not a slight thing when they, who are so fresh from God, love us.

CHARLES DICKENS

He tends
his flock like
a shepherd:
He gathers
the lambs
in his arms
and carries
them close
to his heart;
he gently leads
those that
have young.

Isaiah 40:11